The
Revealing Story of
Underwear

Katie Daynes

Illustrated by Nilesh Mistry

Fashion expert: Cally Blackman

Reading consultant: Alison Kelly
Roehampton University

Contents

Throughout the book, you'll find new underwear words. If you want to find out what they mean, go to page 61.

Chapter 1

Why wear underwear?

There's more to
underwear than
frilly lace.
It can keep you
warm...

keep you from
getting
embarrassed...

...and it can help to keep your other clothes clean.

Centuries ago, people didn't bathe that often. A layer of underclothes kept their outer clothes slightly cleaner – though it didn't always disguise the smell of their sweaty bodies below.

Underwear can also give a certain shape to clothes. It can help people get the figure they would like.

Through history, fashions have changed from wide hips...

to flat chests...

...to pointy breasts.

5

Most of these shapes would be impossible without some special underwear.

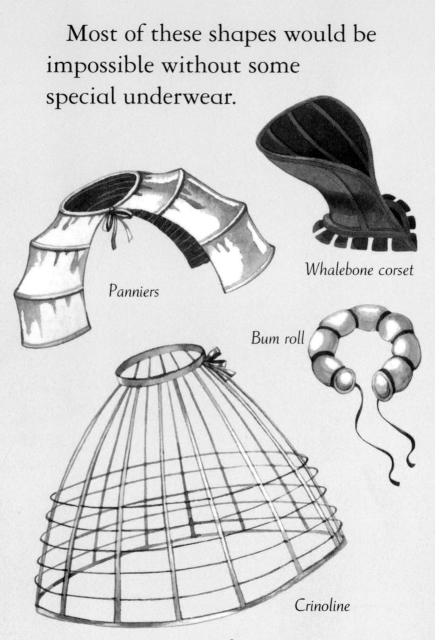

Panniers

Whalebone corset

Bum roll

Crinoline

Chapter 2

Early underwear

The story of underwear begins long ago, in the ancient lands of Egypt, Crete and Rome.

It was scorching hot in Ancient Egypt. People didn't need to wear many clothes and no one wore underwear. Even the Pharaoh, the most important man in Egypt, just wore a little skirt with nothing underneath.

At the public baths in Rome,
the dress code was "wear nothing"
but elsewhere Romans were more
shy about their bodies.

Roman fighters wore a loincloth
and the occasional piece of armor,
while mosaics show women
exercising in the world's first bikinis.

Over time, loincloths grew... up
to the shoulders and down to the
knees. They were renamed tunics.
Tunics were light, airy and great
in the heat. Few people bothered
to wear anything underneath.

10

For the women of Ancient Crete, strips of cloth weren't enough. They wanted very thin waists and high, bare breasts.

The answer was a stiff metal band worn around their waists. This squeezed in their tummies, while pushing up their bosoms. It was painful... but it worked.

Chapter 3

Underwear and panties

Underwear started life in the
Middle Ages – but only for men.
At first they were long, baggy
shorts, known as braies or drawers.
Men wore them under their tunics.

In those days, most people had only one pair of drawers. They were made of wool and very itchy.

With no soap to soften and clean the wool, people even tried using animal dung...

...then splashed on plenty of perfume to disguise the stench.

Rich men owned several pairs of drawers, and they became fancier as expensive fabrics arrived from the East. "We need a pair of drawers underneath," men decided, "to keep our fancy drawers clean."

They renamed the top layer breeches or hose and drawers officially became underwear.

Women didn't wear drawers at all. They simply wore floaty tunics called shifts under their dresses. A stroll in the park could be breezy, but using the toilet was easy.

Some ladies let their shifts peek out at the neck and sleeves. They even added embroidery to make a pretty frill.

In the 17th century, close-fitting
dresses were in fashion. Shifts looked
lumpy underneath, so some women
copied men and wore drawers.

At first, drawers reached below
the knee. Each leg was joined at
the calf, but the seams between the
legs were left wide open. So using
the toilet was still easy.

By Victorian times, everyone was in drawers — though women now wore shifts again as well. The Victorians were obsessed with covering up their bodies.

And polite ladies never mentioned "drawers" in public. They invented code words such as "indescribables" and "unwhisperables" instead.

A few daring women refused to be shy about their underwear. They deliberately wore ankle-length drawers, so the frills would show beneath their dresses.

Men gasped and looked the other way as they walked down the street.

In the 1880s, a very slim figure was fashionable. All-in-one underwear was invented to reduce the bulk of drawers and shifts. It was called the combination.

But fashionable ladies weren't impressed. They soon returned to drawers and shifts.

Knickerbockers

By now, "closed" drawers were catching on. These were drawers with the seams sewn up between the legs. People called them knickerbockers – knickers for short.

During the Second World War, there were lots of shortages. Panties were hard to get hold of, so some women made their own from old curtains or silk from parachutes.

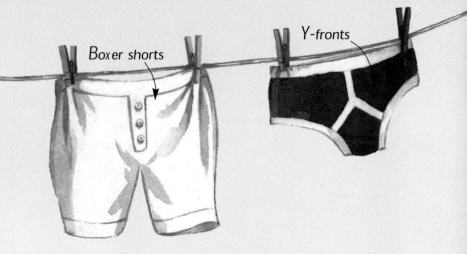

Boxer shorts

Y-fronts

American troops, sent to fight in hot countries, were issued with short army drawers. These were so comfortable, they sparked off a new trend – boxer shorts.

By the 1950s, new materials allowed for closer-fitting, shorter underwear, known as briefs. One design for men was named the Y-front, because of the upside-down "Y" on the front. Openings on either side made it quick to use the toilet.

Today, underwear and panties
are much shorter and tighter –
and they come in every size,
shape and pattern.

Most people go for comfort first,
though there are plenty of frilly,
lacy panties for those who want a
touch of glamour.

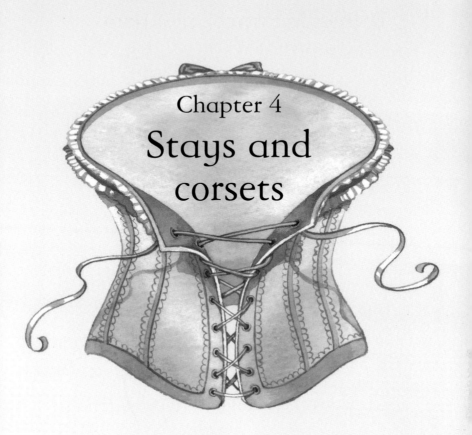

Chapter 4
Stays and corsets

In the 16th century, the age of small waists and curvy hips began. To force their figures into this hourglass shape, women needed special underwear.

23

They didn't know about the metal bands of Ancient Crete. Instead, they tried wearing "bodies" – two figure-hugging layers of cloth, stiffened with paste. These gave the underwear its original name, the bodice.

Bodices were also known as stays, though by the end of the 18th century they were called corsets. This name came from the French word for body, "corps" (say *kor*).

Unfortunately, stiffened paste, cloth and leather wasn't enough to hold in women's flabby waists. Soon strips of wood were sewn into the stays...

then metal...

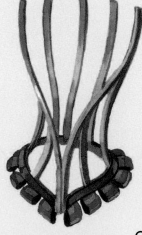

...and even whalebone.

In the 1600s, women also wanted their fronts to be completely flat. So they inserted a "busk" at the front of their stays – a strip of solid horn or whalebone.

It squashed their stomachs and made sitting down extremely awkward.

A hundred years later, the flat look was out and wide hips were in. New corset designs finished at the waist. They had lacing up the back that could be tugged tight.

Women hoped that, by creating tiny waists, it would make their hips look even wider.

Corsets were very popular. But they were also expensive, since each one had to be stitched by hand. Then factories emerged using new machinery. They began to produce ready-made corsets at cheaper prices.

Workers used steam to shape the different sections and joined them together into new designs.

The Victorians found corsets less embarrassing than drawers. Advertisements appeared all around town and corset sales soared.

Graceful form
for sports

Madame Susie's new comfortable sports corset

Soon the choice of designs was enormous, from roomy, pregnancy corsets to flexible sports ones.

Even men forced themselves into tight corsets, desperate to squeeze a few inches off their waistlines. Cartoonists found this very amusing.

By the 1870s, the popular look for women was big bottoms and extremely flat stomachs. But whalebone busks weren't up to it. They broke when people sat down, stabbing them in the stomach.

Steel busks worked better, though the wearers struggled to breathe and fainted regularly.

Doctors were appalled to see girls as young as five wearing rib-cracking corsets. But the obsession with women's waists got worse before it got better...

In the 1890s, every bride wanted a waist no bigger than her age. An 18-year-old would try everything to have an 18 inch (46 cm) waist when walking up the aisle.

Around this time, a corset maker in Paris decided women's lungs were far too squashed. So she designed a health corset with more space for the chest. Women were more than happy to have a fuller bosom.

But they still pulled in their stomachs and the resulting "S" shape was even worse for their health.

In the early 20th century, corsets shrank to just circle the waist. Then a new generation of women rebelled against restrictive clothing. They took off their corsets and put on loose, unwaisted dresses instead.

Some women still wore the small corsets to hold up their stockings or flatten their stomachs, but the tide was turning.

Corsets quickly lost popularity.
Today they are mostly worn by
actresses in period dramas or used
for costumes.

Chapter 5

Petticoats and hoops

The trend for wide hips
created a different
underwear challenge:
how to give
shape to skirts.

Supporting heavy silks and velvets wasn't easy. In the 15th century, tailors made underskirts known as petticoats.

These had to be stiff and wide to puff out the dress fabric on top. If one petticoat wasn't enough, ladies wore two or three.

Some dress designs had a split in the skirt so the top petticoat was on display. But the layers below were hot and heavy.

Luckily, a Spanish invention came to the rescue – a petticoat, reinforced by a framework of cane hoops and named the farthingale.

The Spanish liked a bell-shaped frame.

The French preferred a drum look...

while the English went for a cone design.

Poorer women couldn't afford such elaborate structures. They wore "bum rolls" instead – thick rolls of padding around their hips. Then they hung their skirts over the top.

Bum roll

More slender dress designs in the 17th century forced farthingales out of fashion. Simple, light petticoats replaced big hoops. But hips didn't stay slim for long...

By the 18th century, wide hips were a sign of wealth. Fashionable ladies competed for the widest dress, so a new structure was required.

English tailors came up with a "basket" design – one for each hip. Once again, they preferred a French name, and so the fashion for "panniers" began.

Before long, women looked as if they had an ironing board sewn into their dresses. Simply walking through a doorway took great skill. Some tailors even added hinges to their designs.

Hinge

But moving around was still tricky.

Fifty years later, the bell shape was back and petticoats were stiffer once more. In France, they were called "criardes" (say *cree-ard*). The word meant squawkers, and referred to the noise the petticoats made as women rustled down the street. Cartoonists found this amusing, too.

"Good day, Miss... I say, GOOD DAY, MISS!"

Horse hair ("crin" in French) was an effective way to stiffen petticoats. Horse hair petticoats were known as crinolines, but women sweated under the heavy layers of padding.

So there was a sigh of relief when a new set of hoops was designed. This time they were made of steel and held together by tape. Known as crinoline cages, they were light, cheap and a great success.

In the 1870s, everyone wanted a huge bottom. Crinolines were flattened at the front and sides and the new cage, just at the back, was named a bustle.

Meanwhile, designers were finding extra uses for petticoats. Soft fabric, sewn on at the hem could act as a duster, keeping the rest of the dress clean. And quilted petticoats, stuffed with feathers, were great in cold weather.

Bustle

Duster

44

During the 20th century, cages and hoops disappeared completely, as women opted for a more natural figure. But petticoats are still around... and they're particularly popular at weddings.

Chapter 6

Amazing bras

Through most of history, bras didn't exist. The Greeks and Romans used strips of fabric to support their breasts. After that, people either ignored them or laced them inside a corset.

From the 15th century on, women squeezed themselves up and in, to make their cleavage visible.

As women tugged their waists in tight, their breasts and hips appeared much larger. The curvy look was a hit, so women decided to do more to emphasize their breasts.

In the 1800s, advertisements appeared for bust improvers and "lemon" bosoms. These were pads to stuff inside your corset, made of wool, cotton or rubber.

But when corsets went out of fashion, breasts needed a different kind of support.

For decades, women had been wearing sleeveless tops, known as camisoles, over their corsets. When corsets disappeared, more structure was added to camisoles, and bust bodices were born.

In America, the bust bodice became known as the brassiere, or bra for short. Brassiere was actually the French word for shoulder strap, but nobody seemed to mind.

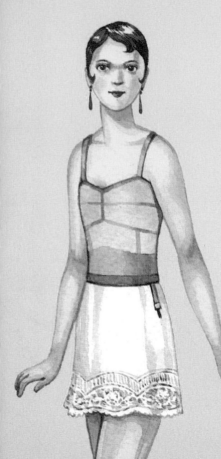

In the 1920s, young women wanted flat chests. They thought this would make them more equal with men. So they wore very tight bras, nicknamed flatteners.

Ten years later, most women had decided that it was good to be different from men. They wore bras with more structure to make their breasts stand out.

From then on, bras were big business. Hundreds of new designs flooded the market – and today, women are spoiled for choice.

Chapter 7

Underwear on the line

Most people prefer their underwear to be clean and comfortable, but this wasn't always possible.

In medieval times, hot water and soft fabrics were luxuries few could afford. Poor people had to wear the same wool drawers until they fell apart.

Rich people could wear silk or linen. Their underwear was lighter, softer and much more expensive. The French for linen is "lin" which is why fancy underwear is sometimes called lingerie.

For centuries, people washed their dirty underwear in tubs of cold water. They trampled on the clothes to get rid of sweat and dirt.

Chalk powder and alcohol removed the worst stains...

...and urine helped to whiten the fabric.

Then people
wrung out the
underwear and draped
it over a hedge to dry.
In the 1600s, soap became
available, but it only lathered up
in hot water. So people began
warming huge copper pots of
washing water over a fire.

They heated heavy stones to smooth out creases in their clothes, until shaped pieces of iron were introduced.

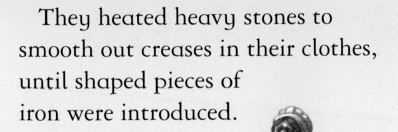

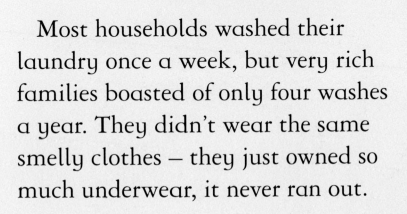

Most households washed their laundry once a week, but very rich families boasted of only four washes a year. They didn't wear the same smelly clothes – they just owned so much underwear, it never ran out.

Corsets had always been tricky to clean. In water, the paste dissolved, the cloth rotted and the metal went rusty. Then designs for washable cotton corsets appeared, with removable strips of steel or whalebone.

In the 1800s, machines to spin and weave cotton were invented. Cotton quickly became the preferred fabric for all underwear.

Over the last hundred years,
another fabric has totally
transformed underwear – elastic.
Gone are the days of lengths
of string...

rows of buttons...

...and fiddly
fasteners.

Elastic waistbands and straps are much simpler. Now there's no need for whalebone or steel, since fabrics that contain elastic, such as Lycra, can do all the squeezing you need.

And with more electric washing machines in homes since the 1960s, having clean underwear has never been so easy!

Underwear words

Bodice an early corset, made from two layers of cloth.

Braies loose drawers worn by men in medieval times.

Brassiere the long word for bra.

Breeches male fancy shorts worn over drawers.

Bum roll a thick roll of padding worn around the waist.

Busk a strip of hard material at the front of a corset.

Bust bodice a camisole with more structure.

Bustle a small structure worn to emphasize the bottom.

Camisole a loose sleeveless top.

Combination all-in-one underwear.

Corset tight-fitting garment worn to narrow the waist.

Criardes thick, stiff petticoats.

Crinoline cage a lightweight frame to support petticoats.

Drawers old-fashioned knee-length underwear.

Farthingale a petticoat reinforced with framework.

Flattener a bra used to flatten the breasts.

Knickerbockers the long name for knickers.

Lemon bosom pads to stuff inside your corset.

Loincloth a garment worn around the loins.

Pannier basket-like structure worn on the hips.

Shift a long, floaty tunic.

Stays an early word for corset.

Y-fronts briefs with a y-shaped opening at the front.

Underwear timeline

4,000 years ago

3,500 years ago

2,500 years ago

1700s

1600s

1800s

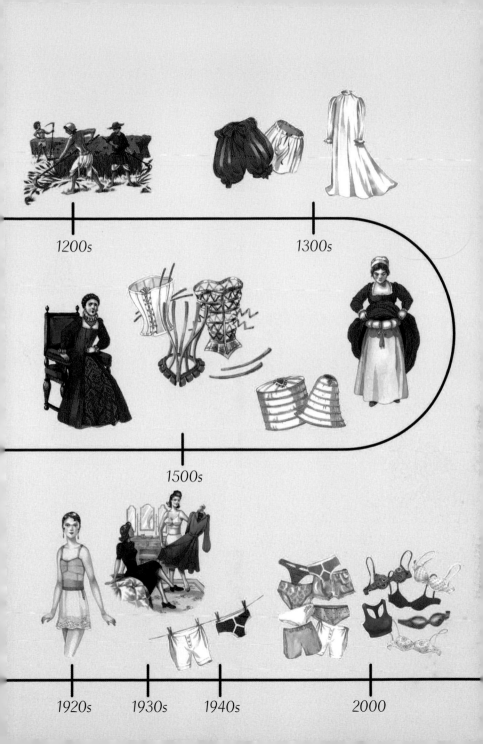

1200s

1300s

1500s

1920s   1930s   1940s   2000

Series editor: Lesley Sims
Editorial assistance: Kate Knighton
Designed by Amanda Gulliver and Zoe Waring
Cover design by Andrea Slane